Sports Illustrated KIDS

BASKETBALL Jokes

by Blake Hoena

illustrated by Daryll Colins

STONE ARCH BOOKS
a capstone imprint

Sports Illustrated Kids All-Star Jokes
is published by Stone Arch Books, a Capstone imprint
1710 Roe Crest Drive
North Mankato, Minnesota 56003
www.mycapstone.com

Sports Illustrated Kids is a trademark of Time Inc.
Used with permission.

Cataloging-in-Publication data is available
on the Library of Congress website.

ISBN: 978-1-4965-5091-0 (library binding)
ISBN: 978-1-4965-5095-8 (eBook pdf)

Summary: SPORTS ILLUSTRATED KIDS presents an all-star collection of
BASKETBALL jokes, riddles, and memes! With slam-dunk one-liners like
"Why do babies make good basketball players? Because they're so good at
dribbling!" these colorful, illustrated joke books will have BASKETBALL fans
rolling in the stadium aisles.

Designer: Brann Garvey

Photo Credits:
Sports Illustrated: Al Tielemans, 34, Damian Strohmeyer, 24, David E. Klutho,
4, 14, John Biever, 28, John W. McDonough, 46, Robert Beck, 40, 57

Printed and bound in Canada.
010382F17

CONTENTS

When the teacher says
it's time for recess...

CHAPTER 1
Full-Court Laughs

Why are basketball players
messy eaters?

They're always dribbling.

What do you get when you
cross a basketball team with
cinnamon crullers?

Dunkin' donuts!

Why do basketball players
love cookies?

Because they can
dunk them.

Why do basketball players
love donuts?

The same reason they
love cookies — duh!

Why is basketball such
a gross sport?

Because players dribble
all over the court.

Why did the kangaroo lose
the basketball game?

He ran out of bounds!

What did the triangle offense
say to the basketball?

You're pointless.

Why didn't the basketball team
have a website?

They couldn't string
three Ws together.

What kind of stories are told
by basketball players?

Tall tales.

Why did the basketball player
visit the bank?

His checks were
all bouncing.

What's the difference
between a ball hog and time?

Time passes.

Why are kangaroos such
great point guards?

They are really good
at bounce passes.

Why are babies good
at basketball?

Because they're
always dribbling!

Why are babies bad
at basketball?

Because they're always
DOUBLE dribbling!

Why did the injured basketball player
only wear a cast for one day?

He had a fast break!

What did the basketball
player say when he was caught
with a finger up his nose?

"I'm practicing my
pick and rolls."

Why did the basketball player
become a big-game hunter?

He liked shooting
three-pointers.

How did the Invisible Man become
an All-Star basketball player?

He had the game's best fadeaway!

When you hand in your homework on time...

CHAPTER 2

Slam Dunk Jokes

What do you call basketball
nets in Hawaii?

Hula hoops!

Why did the basketball
player go to jail?

He shot the ball.

In what sport does a basket get
filled without ever getting full?

Basketball, of course!

Why did the benchwarmer bring a squirt gun to the basketball game?

He wanted to shoot the ball.

What do you call a basketball game where nobody scores?

Pointless.

Why did the ball hog fail fourth grade?

He never passed his tests.

What basketball player smells the nicest?

The scenter (center).

What do you call it when a basketball
player misses an easy shot?

An alley-oops!

What does a basketball player
do before she blows out her
birthday candles?

She makes a swish!

Why did coach let the elephant
play basketball?

He had already broken
the bench.

Why did the basketball player
bring toast to the game?

Because he expected
a lot of jams.

Why did the player host Thanksgiving
at the basketball arena?

She wanted to stuff
the turkey!

Why did the basketball player
become a judge after he retired?

He wanted to stay
on the court.

What do a scrambled egg
and a losing basketball team
have in common?

They've both been beaten.

Why are carpenters the
best rebounders?

They're always
getting boards.

Why can't you play
basketball with pigs?

They hog the ball!

What did the square say
to the basketball?

You're pointless!

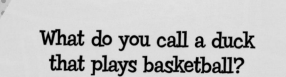

What do you call a duck
that plays basketball?

A slam duck!

How did the basketball team get rid of bees in their arena?

With a buzzer-beater!

Why did the garbage collector get kicked out of the basketball game?

For talking trash.

Why did the team make the point guard wash their plates after lunch?

Because he knew the most about dishes.

Favorite childhood toy? Blocks, of course.

CHAPTER 3

Foul Language

What do you do when you
see a rhino charging in basketball?

Get out of the way!

How did the computer geek foul
out of the basketball game?

I don't know, but it
seemed technical.

Why did the basketball player
bring a suitcase to the game?

Because he was always traveling!

Why was the point guard
called a cheapskate?

Because she was always
taking free throws.

Why did the All-Star center
get called for charging?

Because his credit cards
were over the limit.

Why are baby twins such lousy
basketball players?

They're always
double dribbling!

What's the cheapest part
of a basketball arena?

The free-throw line.

Why did the player sit on the sideline
and sketch pictures of chickens?

He was trying to draw
fowls (fouls).

When the teacher asks who needs to use the restroom..

CHAPTER 4
Fanatic Fans

How do basketball players
stay cool during a game?

They stand near
the fans.

What do basketball cheerleaders
drink before they go to a game?

Root beer!

What are basketball fans
least favorite foods?

Turnovers.

Why is the basketball arena
so hot after the game?

Because all the
fans have left.

Fan #1: Think our team is going
to win this game?

Fan #2: I hoop so!

FAN #1: Our team's just
in transition.

FAN #2: Yeah, it's
going from bad to worse!

Why did the fan send his toddler onto
the basketball court with toys?

Because his team
needed some blocks!

Fan #1: I think our team is trying to build a wall.

Fan #2: Why do you say that?

Fan #1: Look at all the bricks they are throwing!

Fan #1: Does our team have a fight song?
Fan #2: No, but it has a surrender song!

What is the difference between a basketball fan and a baby?

The baby will stop whining after a while.

Where do basketball players wash their socks?

In the bleach-ers.

What do you call a potato at a basketball game?

A spec-tater!

STOP
CELEBRATING!
THE GAME HASN'T
EVEN STARTED!

CHAPTER 5

Rowdy Refs

What does a basketball player
do when he loses his eyesight?

Become a referee!

Why did the referee get fired
from his job?

He kept making
prank calls.

What's the difference between a
potato and a referee?

The potato has eyes!

Why did the chicken cross
the basketball court?

Because the referee
called a foul.

Why didn't the referee blow
his whistle when the
Grizzly charged?

Wouldn't you?!

What do a basketball referee
and a teapot have in common?

They both whistle while
they work.

Why do the Nets always have
the most fouls?

They make things easy to catch.

Why is it hard to find basketball referees?

Because the job is such a tall order!

Why was the referee late
for the game?

He couldn't even
call a cab.

Why did the referee always
carry a phone book?

In case she needed to
make a call.

What did the referee do when he
spotted an elephant charging?

Got out of the way!

Why do basketball referees
never age?

They can reset
the clock.

What's a coach's
favorite color?

Yeller!

What did the referee call a basketball
team chasing a baseball team?

Five after nine.

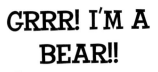

GRRR! I'M A
BEAR!!

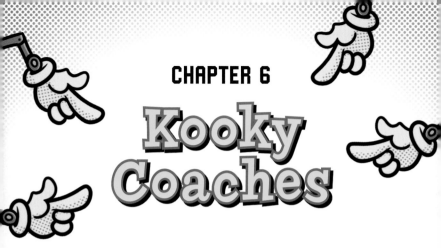

CHAPTER 6

Kooky Coaches

What did the coach say
when his star player missed
the game-winning shot?

Shoot!

Why didn't the nose make
the basketball team?

The coach never picked it.

Why was Cinderella such a
bad basketball player?

Her coach was a pumpkin!

Why did the coach kick Cinderella
off the basketball team?

She kept running away
from the ball!

FAN: Coach, what your team needs is more shooters.

COACH: No, what my teams needs is more makers!

Why did the coach let the rhino start for the basketball team?

Because it broke the bench!

REPORTER: Coach, what do you have to say about your basketball team losing again?

COACH: Well, we are the team to beat!

What are a coach's favorite insects?

Score-pions!

Why did the coach draft a
team full of frogs?

Because they always
make jump shots.

Why did the coach give
her starting player a dollar bill?

She wanted four quarters
out of her!

Why did the coach send his best
player to New York City?

They needed a shot
from downtown.

Why did the coach's team have
trouble on the road?

Because he wasn't a
very good driver.

Why did the coach refuse to take halftime?

He wouldn't accept anything less than the full amount.

Teachers be like...

STOP MONKEYING AROUND!

CHAPTER 7

All-Star Laughs

What do they call professional
basketball in Canada?

The NB-eh!

What do you call a Minnesota
Timberwolves player with an NBA
championship ring?

A thief!

Why did the basketball player
keep walking back and forth?

He was Pacer!

What is Santa's favorite
basketball team?

The New York
St. Knicks!

Basketball tickets can cost
a lot of money, but what team
charges the most?

The Bulls, of course!

What basketball team did
Daniel Boone play for?

The Trail Blazers.

Why did the Washington Wizards
go to Orlando?

To play with the Magic!

What do you call a Memphis
basketball player caught
in the rain?

A drizzly bear!

What do Oklahoma City players
wear under their uniforms?

Thunderwear!

What team is known for always
traveling with the ball?

The Harlem
Globetrotters.

Why do all the Milwaukee
players wear braces?

They have Buck teeth!

Why was Larry Bird like
an angry chicken?

He had a fowl mouth!

Why do the Charlotte Hornets
players all have short hair?

The coach gave
them buzz-cuts!

Why did the Miami Heat win
the championship?

Because they were
always on fire!

Why was the three-year-old
such a big Lakers fan?

He loved Magic.

Why did the barber root for
Los Angeles?

Because he loved
his Clippers!

Why do the Phoenix Suns
have the smartest plays?

They're brighter than
everyone else!

Why did the Mavericks leave
Denver with full stomachs?

Because they ate the
Nuggets for breakfast!

How do you put a Houston
player to sleep?

Rocket.

What are the Lakers'
favorite dessert?

Turnovers!

Why didn't the Raptors
make the playoffs?

They were already
extinct!

Why did the Pelicans get kicked
out a restaurant?

Their bills were
too big.

What do you call a lost Minnesota
basketball player?

A where-wolf!

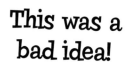

This was a
bad idea!

How to Tell Jokes

1. KNOW the joke.

Make sure you remember the whole joke before you tell it. This sounds like a no-brainer, but most of us have known someone who says, "Oh, this is so funny . . ." Then, when they tell the joke, they can't remember the end. And that's the whole point of a joke — its punch line.

2. SPEAK CLEARLY.

Don't mumble; don't speak too fast or too slow. Just speak like you normally do. You don't have to use a different voice or accent or sound like someone else. (UNLESS that's part of the joke!)

3. LOOK at your audience.

Good eye contact with your listeners will grab their attention.

4. DON'T WORRY about gestures or how to stand or sit when you tell your joke. Remember, telling a joke is basically talking.

5. DON'T LAUGH at your own joke.

Yeah, yeah, I know some comedians break up while they're acting in a sketch or telling a story, but the best rule to follow is not to laugh. If you start to laugh, you might lose the rhythm of your joke or keep yourself from telling the joke clearly. Let your audience laugh. That's their job. Your job is to be the funny one.

6. THE PUNCH LINE is the most important part of the joke.

It's the climax, the payoff, the main event. A good joke can sound even better if you pause for just a second or two before you deliver the punch line. That tiny pause will make your audience mentally sit up and hold their breath, eager to hear what's coming next.

7. The SETUP is the second most important part of a joke.

That's basically everything you say before you get to the punch line. And that's why you need to be as clear as you can (see 2 above) so that when you finally reach the punch line, it makes sense!

8. YOU CAN GET FUNNIER.

It's easy. Watch other comedians. Listen to other people tell a joke or story. Check out a good comedy show or film. You can pick up some skills simply by seeing how others get their comedy across. You will absorb it! And soon it will come naturally.

9. Last, but not least, telling a joke is all about TIMING.

That means not only getting the biggest impact for your joke, waiting for the right time, giving that extra pause before the punch line — but it also means knowing when NOT to tell a joke. When you're among friends, you can tell when they'd like to hear something funny. But in an unfamiliar setting, get a "sense of the room" first. Are people having a good time? Or is it a more serious event? A joke has the most funny power when it's told in the right setting.

BLAKE HOENA

Blake Hoena grew up in central Wisconsin. In his youth, he wrote stories about robots conquering the moon and trolls lumbering around the woods behind his parents' house. He now lives in St. Paul, Minnesota, with his wife, two kids, a dog, and a couple of cats. Blake continues to make up stories about things like space aliens and superheroes, and he has written more than 70 chapter books, graphic novels, and joke books for children.

DARYLL COLLINS

Daryll Collins is a professional illustrator in the areas of magazine & newspaper illustration, children's books, character design & development, advertising, comic strips, greeting cards, games, and more! His clients range from Sports Illustrated Kids and Boys' Life magazine to McDonald's and the US Postal Service. He currently lives in Kentucky.

Joke Dictionary!

bit (BIT)—a section of a comedy routine

comedian (kuh-MEE-dee-uhn)—an entertainer who makes people laugh

headliner (HED-lye-ner)—the last comedian to perform in a show

improvisation (im-PRAH-vuh-ZAY-shuhn)—a performance that hasn't been planned; "improv" for short

lineup (LINE-uhp)—a list of people who are going to perform in a show

one-liner (WUHN-lye-ner)—a short joke or funny remark

open mike (OH-puhn MIKE)—an event at which anyone can use the microphone to perform for the audience

punch line (PUHNCH line)—the words at the end of a joke that make it funny or surprising

shtick (SHTIK)—a repetitive, comic performance or routine

segue (SEG-way)—a sentence or phrase that leads from one joke or routine to another

stand-up (STAND-uhp)—a stand-up comedian performs while standing alone on stage

timing (TIME-ing)—the use of rhythm and tempo to make the joke funnier

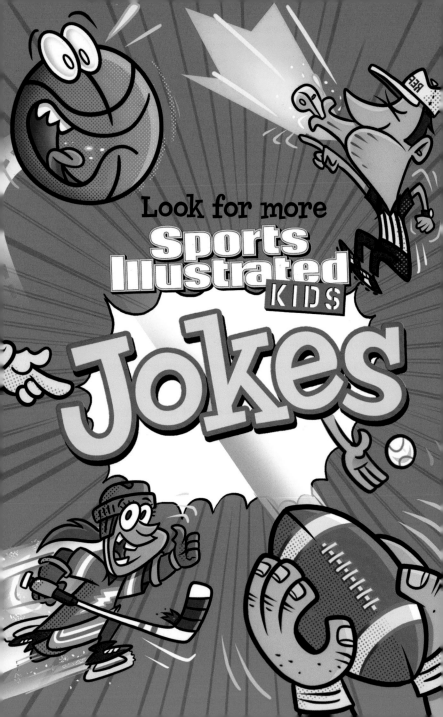

Look for more **Sports Illustrated KIDS Jokes**

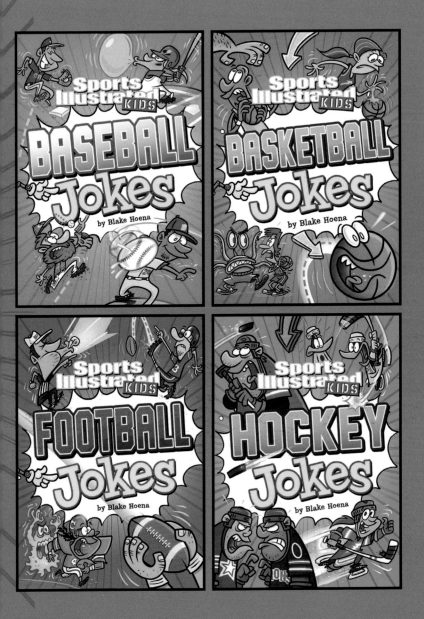

FACTHOUND

Use FactHound to find Internet sites related to this book.

Visit www.facthound.com

Just type in 9781496550910 and go.

www.FactHound.com

Super-cool stuff!

Check out projects, games and lots more at
www.capstonekids.com